P9-DEY-865

BLACK HOLES

ENERGY

GALAXIES

GRAVITY

LIGHT

MYSTERIES OF THE UNIVERSE

MASS & MATTER

SPACE & TIME

STARS

MYSTERIES OF THE UNIVERSE

Galaxies

BILL McAULIFFE

CREATIVE EDUCATION

McLEAN COUNTY UNIT #5
105-CARLOCK

Published by Creative Education
P.O. Box 227, Mankato, Minnesota 56002
Creative Education is an imprint of The Creative Company
www.thecreativecompany.us

Design and production by Blue Design
Art direction by Rita Marshall
Printed in the United States of America

Photographs by Getty Images (Margaret Bourke-White/Time Life
Pictures, Digital Vision, NASA/Space Frontiers/Hulton Archive, Jay M.
Pasachoff, Vladimir Piskunov, SSPL, Stock Montage, Universal History
Archive), iStockphoto (Cristian Andrei Matei, Aaron Rutten), NASA
(NASA, NASA/CXC/SAO/STScI, NASA/ESA, NASA/ESA/Hubble Heritage/
ESA/Hubble Collaboration/A. Evans, NASA/ESA/Hubble Heritage Team,
NASA/ESA/Hubble SM4 ERO Team, NASA/JPL-Caltech, NASA/JPL-
Caltech/STScI)

Cover and folio illustration © 2011 Alex Ryan

Copyright © 2013 Creative Education
International copyright reserved in all countries. No part of this book may
be reproduced in any form without written permission from the publisher.

Library of Congress Cataloging-in-Publication Data
McAuliffe, Bill.
Galaxies / by Bill McAuliffe.
p. cm. — (Mysteries of the universe)
Includes bibliographical references and index.
Summary: An examination of the science behind the astronomical
phenomena known as galaxies, including relevant theories and history-
making discoveries as well as topics of current and future research.
ISBN 978-1-60818-188-9
1. Galaxies—Juvenile literature. I. Title.

QB857.3.M33 2012
523.1'12—dc23   2011040140

First Edition
9 8 7 6 5 4 3 2 1

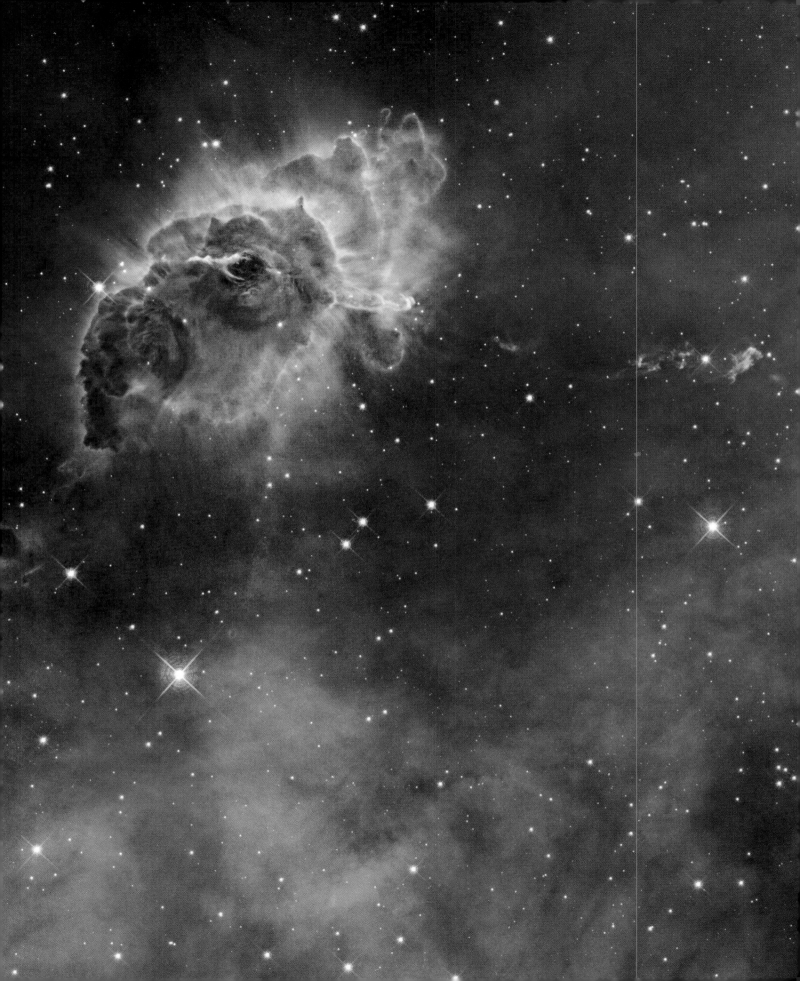

Italian astronomer Galileo Galilei, circa 1610

TABLE OF CONTENTS

Many more stars exist than can be seen in the sky

INTRODUCTION

For most of human history, the true nature of the universe was shrouded in myth and mystery. About 400 years ago, scientists began unraveling those mysteries. Their efforts were so successful that American **physicist** Albert Michelson wrote in 1894, "The more important fundamental laws and facts of physical science have all been discovered, and these are now so firmly established that the possibility of their ever being supplemented in consequence of new discoveries is exceedingly remote." William Thomson, Baron Kelvin, perhaps that era's most famous physicist, echoed Michelson: "There is nothing new to be discovered in physics now. All that remains is more and more precise measurement." Both men were wrong. Within a few years, scientists had revealed the makeup of the tiny **atom** and the unexpected vastness of outer space. Yet the universe doesn't yield its mysteries easily, and much remains to be discovered.

Galaxies are among those elusive mysteries, and as **astronomers** have learned more about galaxies, they have found more questions. When it was discovered that the Milky Way wasn't the only galaxy in the heavens, people started to wonder just how many there were. What makes galaxies move? What holds them together? Do they develop and change in predictable ways? Might any of them contain a small solar system with a tiny planet like ours, with life we might recognize? Unlocking the answers to such questions would not only profoundly affect science but would also necessarily redefine humanity's place in the universe.

British physicist Baron Kelvin, circa 1890

THE ISLAND UNIVERSES

O n a moonless night, far away from the lights of any city, one can scan the heavens and see about 2,000 stars, plus a few planets. Beyond them, it seems, is only the vast, black background of space. But astronomers believe there are 300 sextillion stars in the universe. That's an actual number: 300 followed by 21 zeroes. It means that, for every star we can see above and around us, there are more than 150 million billion others. Most of them are beyond the range of even the most high-powered telescopes. And they're not isolated like the stars we can see. Instead, they're arranged into billions of vast collections of stars called galaxies. Galaxies move through space at astonishing speeds, sometimes colliding like clouds, all the while recycling the basic materials of the **cosmos** into new stars. We don't see much of the spectacle, but astronomers are continually searching for galaxies, from which they hope to learn some of the deepest secrets of the universe.

The visible parts of galaxies are dust, stars, and gas (primarily hydrogen and helium), held together by **gravity** and working together much like an **ecosystem**, each part dependent on the other. Scientists believe a mysterious substance called dark matter and a force called dark energy make up most of a galaxy's content. But the visible material is what galaxies use to make stars. When a galaxy's gases intensely compress, or squeeze together, the **nuclei** of many of the atoms of gas collide and stick together in a process called fusion. This creates not just the star but the star's light as well. It also manufactures new **elements**. Billions of years later, the process might reverse, and the same star might explode in a sudden brightening known as a supernova. This releases material back into space, and the process can repeat itself—often billions of times in the same galaxy.

Almost all stars in the universe are part of one galaxy or another. Large galaxies have been formed by collisions or mergers with smaller galaxies over billions of years.

A pixelated satellite image of a supernova

II

Earth is only one component of the Milky Way

All the stars we can see from Earth are in our home galaxy, the Milky Way, which the ancient Chinese called a silver river. It gets its light from as many as 400 billion stars, including our sun. The sun and all the planets in our solar system are located in an arm of the galaxy that is fairly distant from the center. From where we stand, we are looking sideways through the main disk of our galaxy.

The Milky Way is about 100,000 **light years** across. Astronomers express that distance as about 31,000 **parsecs**. To put it into visual terms, if our solar system were the size of a quarter, the Milky Way would be bigger than half the United States. But on a starry night, stargazers in the Northern Hemisphere, and people in a few places in the Southern Hemisphere, can see beyond the Milky Way to a neighboring galaxy, Andromeda, 2.3 million light years away. Andromeda is the most distant thing that can be seen with the naked eye. Although it appears to us as a faint smudge, in reality it is twice as wide as the Milky Way.

Andromeda and the Milky Way are members of the Local Group, a collection of about 30 known galaxies in a "neighborhood" of space about 10 million light years across. Andromeda, the Milky Way, and a third galaxy, Triangulum, are the big kids on that block. Due to the force of gravity, most galaxies are pulled into groups and clusters with other galaxies, making them the largest gravity-bound structures known. These collections are in turn connected in an ever-expanding, vast cosmic web, although galaxies within their own groups continue to interact and sometimes collide with each other. Andromeda, which is moving at a rate of about 124 miles (200 km) per second, is expected to collide with the Milky Way in about 2.5 billion years.

No one has actually seen the entire Milky Way. But astronomers believe it has a shape much like Andromeda's—a flat pinwheel, or spiral. The Milky Way also has a "halo," a spherical collection of star clusters and stars that orbit (or move in a curved path around) them. The galaxy closest to the Milky Way is the Canis Major Dwarf, an

The cluster of stars at the Milky Way's center glows brightly

ellliptical mini-galaxy of about a billion stars that was discovered in 2003.

The ellipical galaxy is one of the four basic types of galaxy identified by American astronomer Edwin Hubble in the 1920s. Elliptical galaxies can be circular or football-shaped. They have no arms and little gas and dust. Spiral galaxies are flattened disks with curving arms that include the gas and dust needed for star-making. Barred spirals, in which the graceful arms extend from central bars, like water from a spinning lawn sprinkler, are a third distinct type. Lenticular galaxies have both a flattened disk shape and, when seen sideways, a central bulge, so they can also resemble elliptical galaxies. They are not major star-makers. Hubble called other galaxies without any recognizable shape irregulars. Irregular galaxies tend to be small, with plentiful gas. They are busy star-makers. The Large and Small Magellanic Clouds, close neighbors to the Milky Way and visible primarily across the Southern Hemisphere, are examples of irregular galaxies.

Astronomers have recently determined that the Milky Way has a central bar, which means it's now regarded as a barred spiral. Also, some elliptical galaxies are now known as spheroidal galaxies. So many small, or dwarf, galaxies have this shape that it is the most common in the universe.

Some of the most compelling features of galaxies are things astronomers can't see but that they believe exist. The best-known (but still mysterious) phenomena would be black holes—objects compressed to such a density that their gravitational power prevents even light from escaping. Astronomers can sense black holes' presence with **radio** telescopes, which detect short-wave radiation, such as gamma rays and X-rays. These rays are produced by the tremendous heat generated by a black hole, and they're emitted from "invisible" sources all over the universe. It's believed the Milky Way has a black hole at its center. Fortunately, it doesn't seem to be pulling in matter as forcefully as those in other galaxies. That's a continuing puzzle for scientists but, for now, a relief to Milky Way residents.

Another mystery is why galaxies move the way they do. Scientists have determined that material in the outer arms of the Milky Way moves at the same speed as material closer to the center. (If the material lagged, the galactic spiral would wind up, and it doesn't.) This motion runs contrary to conventional physics—unless some unseen material is exerting a gravitational push and pull on the visible material in a galaxy, that is. Astronomers call this invisible material dark matter. They can't see it, but because something is behaving as visible material would, they believe it exists. Similarly, astronomers have not been able to figure out why galaxies are moving apart faster than they did several billion years ago. Given the laws of gravity, the universe should be slowing its expansion or even collapsing. Something is counteracting gravity, and scientists call it dark energy. In fact, scientists believe that all the matter we can see and measure amounts to only 4 percent of what's in the universe. The rest is dark matter and dark energy, making the universe 96 percent mystery.

GALAXIES

An 1801 artistic representation of the Virgo constellation

EXPANDING UNIVERSE, EXPANDING IDEAS

No one was watching 14 billion years ago when a dense cluster of material, perhaps no bigger than an atom, flew apart in a tremendous explosion. No one was listening, either, although today the event is called the Big Bang—the moment many scientists believe the universe and even space itself came into being.

Fast-forward through all of time to the present. Astronomers striving to learn more about the universe and how it was created know they can get a good idea by looking at galaxies. That's because some galaxies are so far away that the light astronomers see today left the galaxy billions of years ago. It's like an old movie, discovered in a dark attic, that astronomers are seeing for the first time—a chain of events that took place closer and closer to the time of the Big Bang. And because galaxies are filled with stars in all stages of development, astronomers study them to see how stars are created, endure, and die. Understanding more about that process teaches scientists more about the fundamentals of the universe.

It took a long time for people to recognize galaxies at all. When the ancient Greeks looked up to the stars nearly 3,000 years ago, one of the spectacles they admired was the bright band—not quite stars and not quite clouds—that slashed across the heavens. And just as they explained the arrangement of the stars by turning them into the outlines of people and animals we call constellations, so too they conjured up a story explaining the whitish blur in the night sky. It was, they said, milk that the goddess Hera spilled while nursing her son, Heracles. They called it *galaxias kyklos*, which means "milky circle." We know it as the Milky Way, our home galaxy.

For centuries, the Milky Way was thought to be a cloud of gases. But in 1609, Italian mathematics professor and astronomer Galileo Galilei, using a telescope he'd made himself, determined that the Milky Way was a massive collection of individual stars. Galileo's observations also led him to champion the idea that Earth was not at the center of the universe, but it revolved around the sun. Galileo's ideas soon put him in conflict with biblical teachings and the leaders of the Catholic Church, who in 1616 first accused him of **heresy**.

alileo lived the last nine years of his life under house arrest. But his work ultimately stood as a pillar of modern understanding of the universe. And it was his approach to his subject that also marked him as one of history's first and greatest scientists. Galileo used observations and experiments to question what had been established ideas. Such a strategy is the cornerstone of what has since become known as the scientific method. It is still the process by which new understandings in all fields of science—from astronomy to zoology—are gained.

In the 18th century, Immanuel Kant, a German philosopher, described foggy patches in the night sky as "island

We now know that the planets revolve around the sun

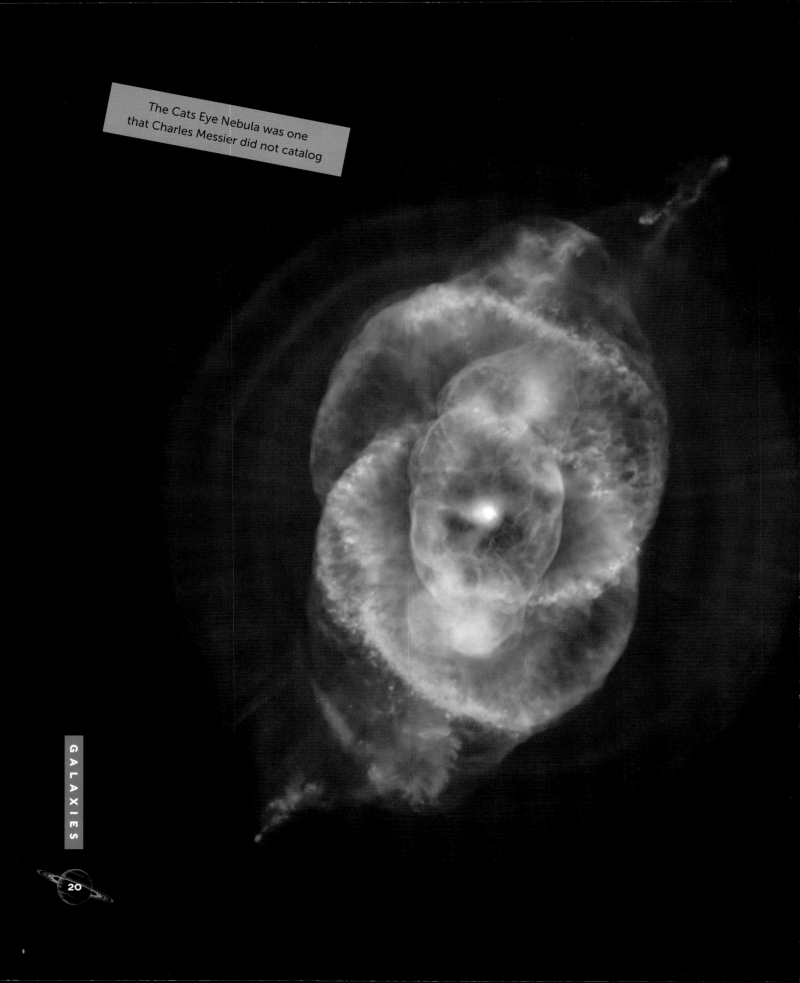

The Cats Eye Nebula was one
that Charles Messier did not catalog

A Redshift in Thinking

of a train whistle has with how astronomers the universe is expanding. f a passing train's whistle pidly as the train roars s because sound travels s the train approaches, of the whistle's sound pressed, and the pitch t passes the listener, gth stretches out, and ops. This is the Doppler ed for Austrian physicist

Christian Doppler (1803–53). Light also travels in waves, so it's also subject to the Doppler Effect. Light with shorter wavelengths is blue or violet, while longer-wavelength light is red. Looking at light from galaxies through a **spectrograph**, American astronomer Vesto Slipher (1875–1969) found that the light was usually concentrated on the red end of the **visible spectrum**. From this "redshift" he concluded that many galaxies were pulling away at

astonishing speeds. Edwin Hubble later determined that those galaxies farthest away were retreating the fastest. Until then, it was believed that the universe would contract due to gravity. The discovery of redshifts reversed that notion and led to the idea of dark energy—an unseen force that counteracts gravity within and among galaxies.

universes." That might have made them seem worth studying, but in France, astronomer Charles Messier found they simply got in the way of his search for comets. Messier began numbering the objects, which he called **nebulae**, in a catalog so that he and other astronomers would know how to avoid them. In 1771, he published an index of 45 "Messier objects," and in time it became one of the most famous and reliable collections of information in the history of astronomy. By 1781, there were 103 objects on the list, but scientists, using Messier's own additional notes, expanded the list to include 110 by 1966, nearly 200 years later. M1 in the catalog is the Crab Nebula, the vivid remnant of an exploding star that was documented by Chinese, Arab, Japanese, and Korean astronomers in A.D. 1054. M31 is the Andromeda galaxy, our nearest galaxy.

EXPANDING UNIVERSE, EXPANDING IDEAS

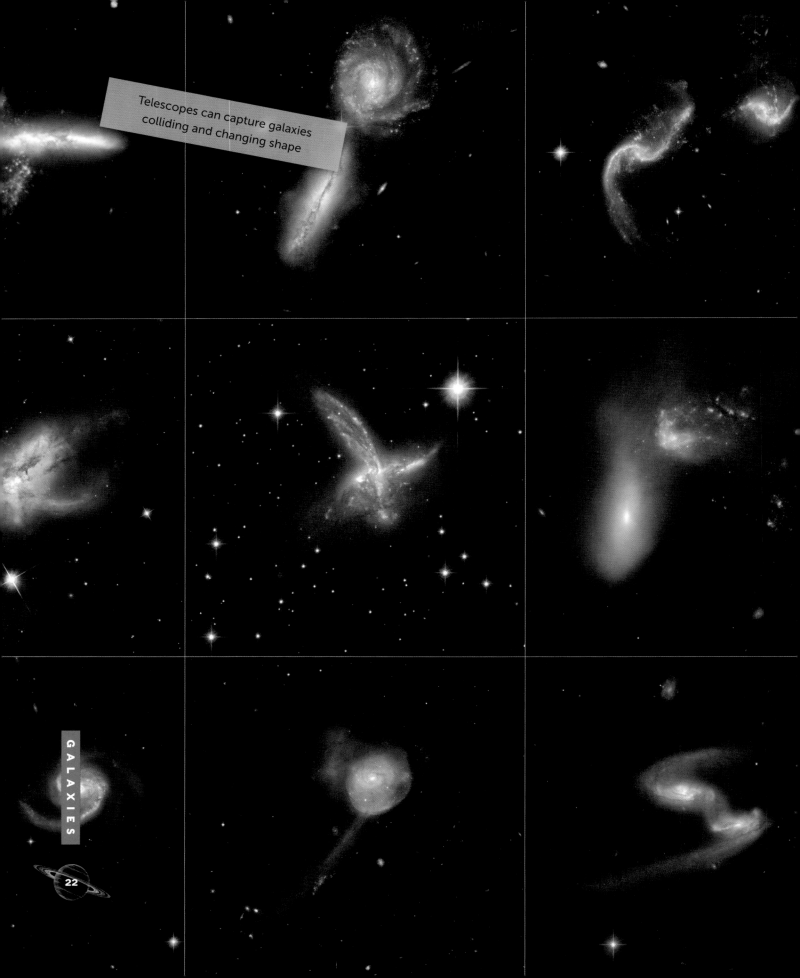

Telescopes can capture galaxies colliding and changing shape

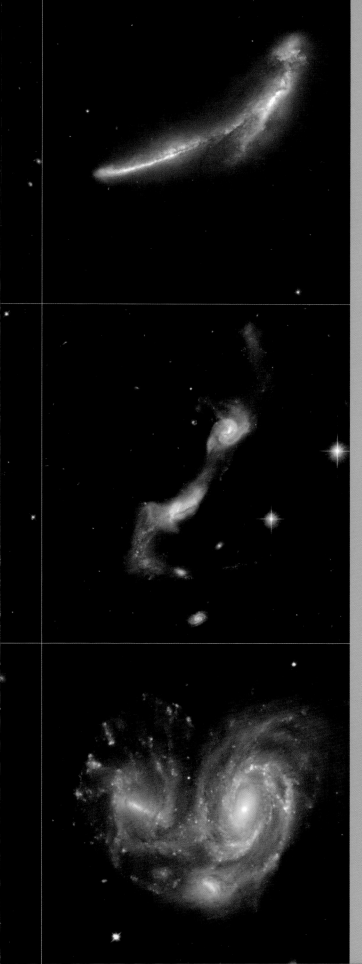

Through the 1800s and into the early 1900s, astronomers continued to use their telescopes to roam deeply and widely throughout space, publishing ever more extensive catalogs of the nebulae. The General Catalogue of Nebulae and Clusters, published in 1864, listed 5,079 objects. The New General Catalogue (NGC), appearing 24 years later, added nearly 3,000 more. The Index Catalogue (IC), a revision of the NGC, published in 1908, listed more than 15,000. Since then, most nebulae have been determined to be galaxies and carry designations from several catalogs. Andromeda, for instance, is notated as both M31 and NGC 224. But tens of thousands have been catalogued, and more are being discovered every day. The Sloan Digital Sky Survey, using a telescope at an observatory in New Mexico, has mapped nearly one million galaxies since the year 2000.

Knowledge of galaxies exploded in the early years of the 20th century.

Astronomers at Yerkes Observatory, built in 1897 in Williams Bay, Wisconsin, determined the spiral nature of the Milky Way and that the galaxy has many stars that are actually concealed by **interstellar** dust. In 1905, German-born scientist Albert Einstein developed the first of his theories of relativity, which showed that, since light always moves at a constant speed, space and time are flexible dimensions. He went further to show that gravity is essentially a warp, or curve, in space and time caused by a mass, or body in space—an idea that clearly demonstrated the possibility of black holes, first suggested a century before. Einstein's theories of relativity became key tools in the study of **astrophysics**.

A short time later, after a new mathematical formula was developed that could measure the distance from Earth to individual stars, astronomer Edwin Hubble determined in the early 1920s that Andromeda was not a nebula but was in fact a galaxy, located millions of light years beyond the Milky Way. As with Galileo's discovery that the universe had more stars than anyone had previously realized, Hubble's calculation also shook the accepted understanding of the size of the universe, making it again far larger than anyone had believed.

Technological advances during and after World War II (1939–45) gave astronomers new ways of "seeing" what was in the universe. Using radio and X-ray detection, **infrared** and **ultraviolet** sensors, and satellites above Earth's obscuring atmosphere, astronomers could identify more than just the visual features and forces in space. Hundreds of galaxies have been discovered by the radio waves they emit rather than by direct visual observations.

In the 1960s, astronomers looking out at the farthest reaches of space were puzzled by some extremely bright objects that also emitted intense radio signals. These "quasi-

The Yerkes Observatory, pictured in 1915

Quasars emit X-ray radiation
from their centers

Where No Man Has Gone Before

Since its first appearance on television in 1966, *Star Trek* has not only inspired a generation of fans, but it has also triggered curiosity about the universe, space travel, technology, the possibility of intelligent life, and cooperation among alien civilizations. By featuring explorations throughout the Milky Way, *Star Trek* also put the galaxy's spiral shape front and center in fans' imaginations. The dominant fleet of starships in the series, including the *Enterprise*, was known as the Galaxy class. The crew's travels were among four quadrants of the galaxy, where black holes were understandably a hindrance to travel. Because of its clever blending of science and fiction, there have been attempts to construct *Star Trek* realities or to strongly suggest that events in *Star Trek* might be possible someday. However, it's unlikely that people will be able to travel to galactic destinations as quickly as they did in *Star Trek,* for instance, without major alterations in the structure of the galaxy. (*Star Trek* characters needed "warp drives" to propel them to new adventures faster than it would actually take.) The Web site Star Trek Cartography (http://www.stdimension.org/int/Cartography/cartography.htm) takes a more educational approach, though, by mapping out how *Star Trek*'s plots might have taken place in the actual Milky Way.

stellar radio sources" quickly became known as "quasars." Soon, scientists determined that they were the centers, or nuclei, of distant galaxies. Quasars are the brightest objects in the universe and are where matter is being rearranged with extreme forces that might have been common shortly after the Big Bang, making our Milky Way seem settled and middle-aged by comparison. Most known quasars are at least 3 billion light years away and receding quickly. The brightest quasar, located deep in the constellation Virgo, gives off 2 trillion times the light energy of the sun. The Sloan Digital Sky Survey has tracked more than 120,000 quasars in all. Both their distance and their brightness suggest that quasars are young by cosmic standards. They are good examples of how the search for galaxies provides new knowledge of what happened billions of years ago.

EXPANDING UNIVERSE, EXPANDING IDEAS

27

Jupiter's four largest moons are called the "Galilean satellites"

TOOLS OF DISCOVERY

For most of history, people gazed at the stars with the only instruments they had available—their eyes. But the discovery of glass, followed by the development of optical telescopes and, more recently, the combination of radio telescopes and space travel, have allowed people to see to the limits of their imaginations. The Roman scholar Lucius Seneca the Younger (4 B.C.–A.D. 65) was the first person known to observe that glass could be used to magnify objects. By the late 1500s A.D., numerous inventors were putting glass lenses into tubes to make the first telescopes. But credit for the invention generally goes to a Dutchman named Hans Lippershey (1570–1619), a lens maker who built a telescope in 1590 for the precise purpose of looking at stars.

Galileo Galilei (1564–1642) used lenses he had made himself to build a refracting telescope that could magnify objects to appear 30 times as large as they appeared to the naked eye. Through it, he was able to see dark, cool spots on the sun's surface and four of Jupiter's moons. He also detected changes in sunlight and shadow on Venus and mountains and craters on the moon.

Several decades later, English mathematician and physicist Isaac Newton (1643–1727) built the world's first reflecting telescope, using mirrors to produce far sharper images of distant objects than the glass lenses in refracting telescopes like Galileo's. Reflecting telescopes became the standard in astronomy. But Newton's fame went beyond telescopes. As a young man, the story goes, he saw an apple fall in his orchard. What made it fall? From that question, Newton established the law of gravity, which states that every bit of mass in the universe is attracted to every other bit. He further demonstrated how gravity determined the orbits of what were then the six known planets and that comets were also traveling in orbits around the sun and thus likely to return. Also, Newton's investigations into how light was composed of seven colors helped shape major discoveries regarding the movements of galaxies nearly three centuries later.

John Herschel followed in his father's footsteps as an astronomer

A German-born British organist and royal astronomer named William Herschel (1738–1822), who discovered the planet Uranus in 1781, received a copy of the Messier catalog of nebulae that same year. Fascinated, he and his sister Caroline (1750–1848) spent the next several decades cataloging other deep-space objects. Ultimately, they described more than 2,000. The Herschels even tried to map the Milky Way, which they regarded as the entire universe, putting the sun at the center. The view of the Milky Way through telescopes in the late 18th and early 19th centuries was obscured by dust, so there was no way to see to its distant edges. But the Herschels' catalog hinted at the many mysteries even beyond what they could observe.

German Robert Bunsen (1811–99) may be known to all chemistry students as the inventor of the Bunsen burner. However, he didn't invent it—he adapted an earlier device—and, in fact, one of his greatest contributions to science was not in the field of chemistry but in astronomy. In about the 1830s, scientists determined that light given off by a metal and passed through a prism would give off a pattern unique to that metal. In 1859, Bunsen and fellow German Gustav Kirchhoff (1824–87) found that, by using the same technique, they could establish which elements made up the sun and stars. Soon, the approach, known as spectral analysis, combined with photography to produce new breakthroughs in astronomical observation. English astronomer William Huggins (1824–1910) used spectral analysis in 1864 to determine that some nebulae were indeed just gas, as they had appeared for centuries, while others were vast collections of individual stars. Other scientists employed spectral analysis to probe into the strange and distant corners of the universe, finding that objects in deep space were actually made of many of the same materials as Earth.

A decisive step in determining that nebulae were galaxies was an indirect discovery made by Harvard University astronomer Henrietta Leavitt (1868–1921). In 1912, while studying stars in the Magellanic Clouds whose brightness varied, Leavitt found a clear relationship between a star's luminosity, or the amount of energy it emits, and its

Herschel's reflecting telescope was mounted on a wheeled platform

Edwin Hubble at the Mount
Wilson Observatory, 1937

rhythmic changes in brightness, which is the light that reaches us on Earth. That, in combination with some known mathematical formulas regarding light, made it possible to calculate the distances between Earth and stars.

Only 12 years later, in 1924, Edwin Hubble (1889–1953) noticed some regularly blinking stars in Andromeda. Using Leavitt's "Period-Luminosity Law," Hubble determined that Andromeda was nearly one million light years beyond the Milky Way. That discovery forced scientists to realize that the universe might be far larger than they had ever imagined. Hubble then expanded even on that idea. In 1929, as he was measuring the speeds at which galaxies were moving by how they appeared when viewed through a **spectroscope**, Hubble determined that the universe was not only big but that it was getting bigger. In fact, galaxies were moving away faster than they had been millions of years before. And the most distant galaxies, he found, were accelerating the fastest.

Through much of the 20th century, astronomers joined with rocket scientists to try to get beyond Earth's atmosphere for better views of space. The atmosphere is always moving, which makes stars appear to twinkle—a charming feature to most onlookers but a frustration for scientists who would prefer a clear and steady view. The atmosphere also blocks certain types of radiation, such as ultraviolet, infrared, gamma rays, and X-rays, which are keys to identifying the makeup, temperature, and dynamics of many bodies in space.

In the 1970s, astronomers began attaching telescopes to high-flying jets and rockets and detected numerous sources of infrared light in outer space. Today, some of the most dramatic images of galaxies and other spectacles in deep space are from telescopes in space itself. The best known of those is the Hubble Space Telescope, named for Edwin Hubble.

The Hubble Space Telescope, developed by both the National Aeronautics and Space Administration (NASA) and the European Space Agency, was launched in 1990. Despite several breakdowns over the years that required visits from astronauts to repair, Hubble has sent back a rich collection of images. These images have helped astronomers determine the age of the universe more accurately than ever before. They have helped identify quasars and the existence of dark energy, and, by seeing farther across space than ever before, have shown the universe as it was when it was young. That has given astronomers a greater understanding of how galaxies form. Recent observations of the elliptical galaxy NGC 4150, for instance, showed evidence that the galaxy had recently collided with a dwarf galaxy, triggering a burst of star formation. Elliptical galaxies have long been thought to consist only of old stars, but the recent Hubble observation could change that thinking. Scientists are discovering that collisions between galaxies are quite common and are probably the way most of the large galaxies—including the Milky Way—came to be. Astronomers also recently used data collected by Hubble to determine that dwarf galaxies create stars in more places and over much longer periods than ever believed, another step forward in galactic knowledge.

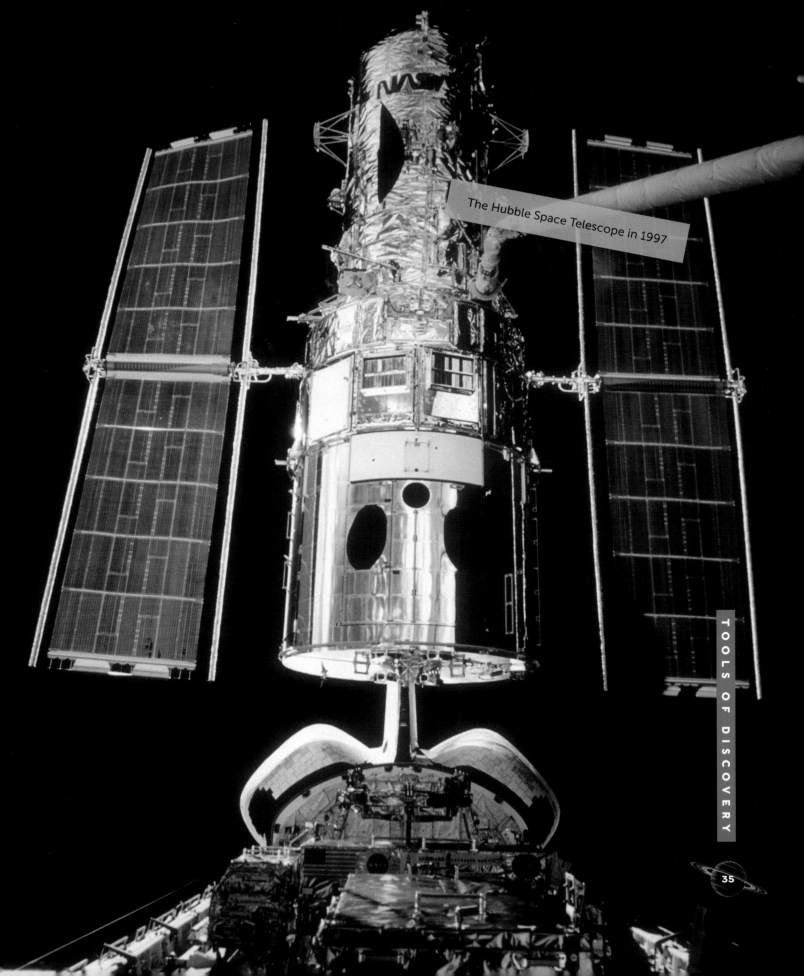

The Hubble Space Telescope in 1997

The Orion Nebula could contain more than 1,000 young stars

WAY BACK TO THE FUTURE

Like **paleontologists** and **archaeologists**, astronomers study the past. But their goal is to learn about more than just history on Earth. Astronomers are trying to uncover secrets about the universe itself, which means peering back to a time well before Earth even existed. Just seeing stars, galaxies, and other objects during the process of their creation isn't an end in itself. By tracking those fundamental events and assessing the forces and materials that both caused and resulted from them, astronomers can learn about life on Earth. Some of the things they might learn include how we got here, what we're made of, whether there might be other beings like us, and how long we're likely to last. Indeed, the farther back astronomy goes, the more it advances.

Tremendous strides have been made in astronomy in recent years, with the development of space-based telescopes and sophisticated radiation detection tools. With an increasing number of scientists from around the world launching probes and comparing their findings, the pace of research is accelerating ever more rapidly. Humans have been studying space for thousands of years, but it's been less than a century since we even knew ours wasn't the only galaxy in the universe. Today, in the early years of the 21st century, researchers have already detected objects and events 13.1 billion light years away. That's getting close to the edge of the universe, but because that edge continues to pull farther away, glimpsing it is an elusive goal. Scientists are determined to keep searching and learning more, not only about the limits of the cosmos but about the many unknowns closer to home.

The Hubble Space Telescope, which has accomplished thousands of breakthroughs in space science and sightseeing, is expected to fall out of Earth orbit in 2013. Its dramatic work will be carried on by the James Webb Space Telescope (JWST). JWST was named for James E. Webb, NASA's chief from 1961 to 1968—key years in the agency's historic program to put a person on the moon. The telescope has been developed through a partnership involving 17 countries, with NASA, the European Space Agency, and the Canadian Space Agency taking the lead.

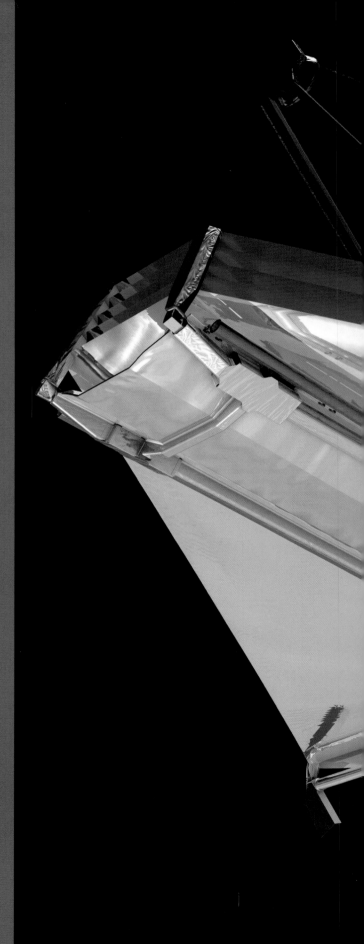

Scheduled for launch in 2018, JWST will explore space from an orbit 940,000 miles (1.5 million km) from Earth—nearly 2,600 times farther into space than Hubble. Equipped with a 21.6-foot-wide (6.5 m) mirror covered with a thin sheet of gold, JWST will also be able to examine far broader areas of space. The telescope will detect primarily infrared images, helping it "see" objects that are obscured by dust or are so far away and receding so quickly that their light waves have been stretched beyond the visible into infrared wavelengths. Also, by examining small groups of stars in different stages of development in galaxies, JWST will focus on the **evolution** of galaxies, assess the elements found in them, and trace the

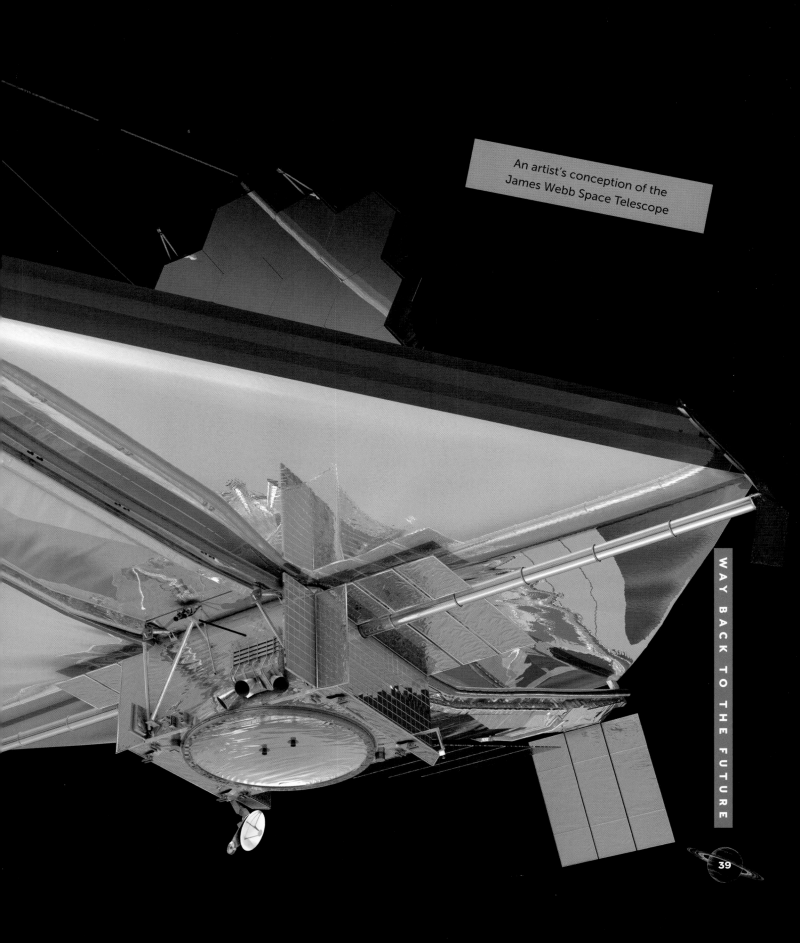

An artist's conception of the
James Webb Space Telescope

Satellites orbit Earth for many purposes

The Handy Black Hole

...were imagined by ... in the 18th century, ...them "dark bodies." ... "black hole" wasn't ...e 1960s. Since then, ...e possibly the most ...astronomical term in ...uage, surpassing even ..."quasar" (which until ...had been a television ...'galaxy," a long-popular ...erican car. That may ...he term so vividly describes a place where all things (even light) disappear. As such, it can be used to suggest a trap, forgetfulness, and disorderliness, and politicians have used it to describe government programs they regard as wasteful. But the term is also used to convey energy or menace. An area of Oakland-Alameda County Coliseum, home of the black-and-silver-clad Oakland Raiders professional football team, is designated as The Black Hole, where the most passionate and vocal fans sit. The name has been used for everything from roller coasters and pinball games to movies and songs, usually with themes of **alienation**, mystery, or loss. But as it's popularly understood, the term is probably misused. A black hole isn't really a "hole" at all. It's an extremely dense object with tremendous gravitational force. Just don't get too close.

exchanges between those elements and the gas and dust in the galaxies. It will also enable astronomers to re-examine the theory that large galaxies are created by collisions of smaller ones and to try to establish the apparent links between galaxies' growth and development of black holes at their centers.

X-ray telescopes, gamma ray detectors, ground- and space-based radio receivers, networks of satellites, and even old-fashioned (but extremely advanced) optical telescopes will also be involved in addressing many of the current mysteries in the universe. Some are already in use. Others, like the Atacama Large Millimeter/submillimeter Array in Chile, are coming online today. This device, involving research agencies from Europe, the U.S., Canada, Chile, Japan, and Taiwan, is an **interferometer** with 66 telescopes, which will detect a type of infrared light that can penetrate Earth's atmosphere. Construction began in 2003 on a desert plateau in the Andes Mountains at 17,030 feet (5,190 m) above sea level, where the instruments' receptivity will be enhanced by the dry air and thin atmosphere. It is expected to be completed in 2013. Meanwhile, NASA's Wide-field Infrared Survey Telescope, which will prowl through space studying dark energy and other solar systems, isn't expected to get off the ground until 2020.

Going into the 2010s, astronomers are concentrating their energies on a few central questions: How do gas, stars, planets, elements, and even life forms cycle through galaxies, and what happens to them while they're there? How do matter and energy flow around and through galaxies? How do black holes develop, and what impact do they have on their surroundings? Can we reach an explanation, understanding, and description of dark energy and dark matter?

lack holes will be at the heart of much of the coming research, just as they are at the centers of galaxies themselves. Astronomers know that galaxies quickly grow black holes in their nuclei with masses that can equal a billion suns. But one current mystery is which came first—the galaxy or the black hole? Might black holes be the engines that condense the gases in space into galaxies and stars, attracting the gases with their tremendous gravitational pulls? Or do other forces within a galaxy give rise to a black hole? Astronomers hope to find the answers to such questions and perhaps even develop the ability to map the process. Similarly, researchers hope to find ways of examining changes in gravitational forces across the universe from the mergers of black holes in galaxies. This would help reveal more about the very architecture and mechanics of the universe.

Astronomers have also been drawn in recent years to dwarf galaxies. Since 2009, astronomers using Hubble Space Telescope data have determined that elliptical galaxies, long thought to have used up much of their star-making material, apparently resume those operations after collisions with dwarf galaxies. They've also found that dwarf galaxies make stars over much broader areas and for much

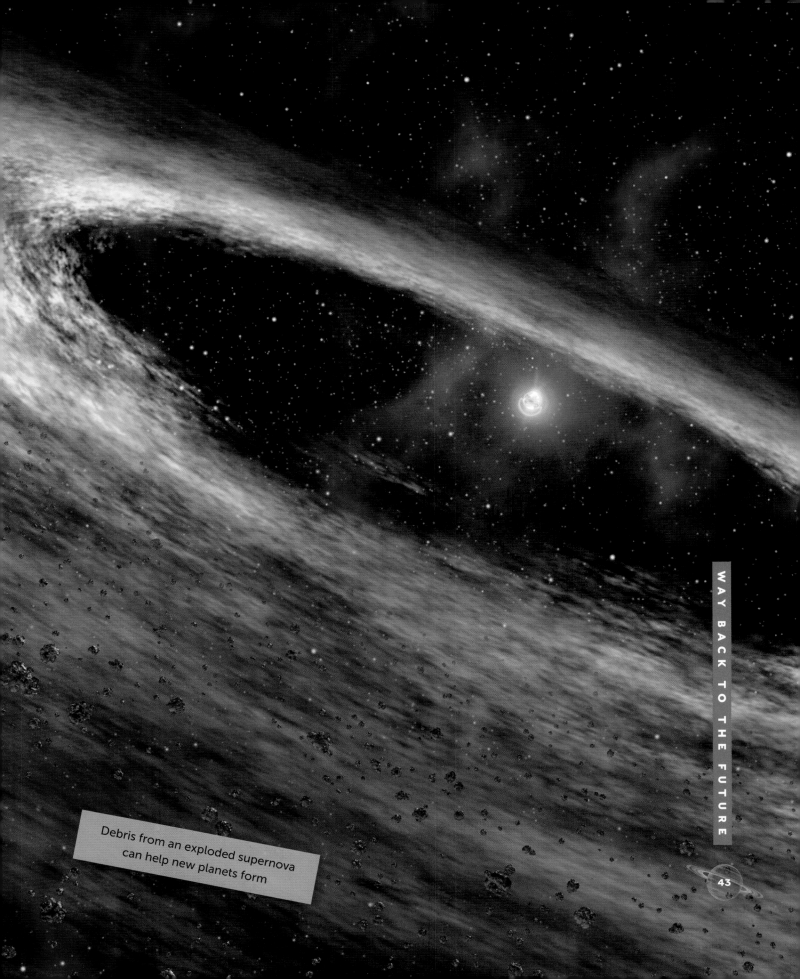

Debris from an exploded supernova can help new planets form

43

Astronomical research is becoming increasingly international in scope, and the European Organization for Nuclear Research is turning up in a lead role. Its **acronym**, CERN, comes from its original French name, Conseil Européen pour la Recherche Nucléaire. The organization was founded in 1954 to bring scientists in western Europe together to study the basic structures of the universe, conducting research that, according to CERN's own mission statement, is not prompted by military interests. Today, more than 60 nations have come together through CERN to operate the Large Hadron Collider (LHC). The LHC is a device that forces tiny particles called hadrons to collide at extremely high energy in a tube laid out in a circle 17 miles (27 km) in diameter and 328 to 574 feet (100–175 m) underground along the border between France and Switzerland. The collisions create types of matter scientists believe are similar to those that existed in the universe a fraction of a second after the Big Bang. Researchers hope the results might help them to better understand gravity and the structure of space and time, as well as to discover more conclusive evidence of dark matter. Such research has led to four Nobel Prizes in Physics for CERN scientists in 1976, 1984, 1988, and 1992.

longer periods of time. Both are indications that, as our universe ages, it's also rejuvenating itself.

Indeed, just as stargazing was fundamental to ancient religions, cultures, and science, so it remains central to today's efforts to understand the universe. Stars in galaxies represent a sort of **fossil record** of the universe. Studying them can reveal how galaxies form, endure, merge, and transform and how the basic elements of our world came to be.

The ongoing and energetic inquiry should lead to a better understanding of how the first galaxies formed after the Big Bang and how that development might be continuing in our own Milky Way. It may give us ways to test gravity itself, and to find out, by observing processes that can't be duplicated in any Earth-bound laboratory, whether

The Tadpole Galaxy's "tail" is about 280,000 light years long

gravity indeed operates by a universal law or works differently in the undiscovered environments of deep space. The quest may even guide us to find other life in the universe.

In 2010, the National Research Council reported to the U.S. Congress on the state of space studies and the roads researchers are about to take. The agency expressed confidence that scientists probing the galaxies are about to uncover many of the secrets of the cosmos. But it also suggested there could be surprises. "We anticipate the discovery of the wholly unanticipated," the report noted. With the speed of research continuing to increase, it should be an exciting ride through the galaxies, filled with many revelations and ever more mysteries.

ENDNOTES

acronym — a word formed from the first letters of other words in a name

alienation — a sense of being isolated or cut off from support and understanding

archaeologists — people who study human history, primarily by excavating sites and examining what people left behind

astronomers — people engaged in the scientific study of planets, stars, and other celestial phenomena

astrophysics — the branch of astronomy that deals with the behavior, movement, and other physical properties of stars and other celestial bodies

atom — the smallest part of an element with the chemical properties of that element

cosmos — the universe seen as a whole

ecosystem — a community of plants, animals, and other living things and the landscape in which they interact

elements — the basic parts from which all substances are formed

evolution — the process by which something changes over time from one stage to another

fossil record — evidence of the history of life on Earth, presented through the remains of organisms preserved in rock

gravity — the force of attraction between all masses in the universe, which causes objects on Earth to fall toward the center of the earth, and which keeps the moon in steady orbit around Earth and the planets in orbit around the sun

heresy — a belief or idea that is not accepted, according to the teachings of an organized religion

infrared — a type of light that cannot be seen by human eyes; its wavelength is longer than visible light's

interferometer — a device that receives a signal from a single source from two different angles and combines them

interstellar — between stars

light years — the distance light travels in a year, which is 5.9 trillion miles (9.5 trillion km)

nebulae — bright clouds of dust and gases in space, and the former term for galaxies; a single such cloud is a nebula

nuclei — more than one nucleus, which is the core of an atom that contains positively charged protons and noncharged neutrons

optical — of or relating to sight or visible light

paleontologists — people who study prehistoric life through fossilized animals and plants

parsecs — scientific measurements of distance equal to 3.3 light years, or 19.5 trillion miles (31.2 trillion km)

physicist — a person who studies matter and motion through space and time in an effort to discover the physical laws of the universe

radio — relating to the longest electromagnetic waves of energy, which are distinct from waves of visible light and can't be seen

refracting — operating by bending light

spectrograph — an image of the electromagnetic spectrum of a light source

spectroscope — an instrument that separates a light wave into different frequencies, isolating the colors that comprise white light

ultraviolet — a type of light that is invisible to the human eye and has a shorter wavelength than visible light

visible spectrum — the wavelengths of light that can be seen by the human eye; they are part of the electromagnetic spectrum, which includes invisible gamma rays, X-rays, microwaves, ultraviolet, infrared, and radio waves

WEB SITES

Amazing Space: The Star Witness News
http://amazing-space.stsci.edu/news/
Keep up with all the latest "tele-scoops" from the Hubble Space Telescope through this online newspaper.

Ask an Astrophysicist: Milky Way and Other Galaxies
http://imagine.gsfc.nasa.gov/docs/ask_astro/galaxies.html
Get all your galactic questions answered here, and find new resources for further research.

SELECTED BIBLIOGRAPHY

Asimov, Isaac. *The Milky Way and Other Galaxies.* Milwaukee, Wisc.: Gareth Stevens Publishing, 2005.

Canadian Space Agency. "James Webb Space Telescope, Successor to Hubble." http://www.asc-csa.gc.ca/eng/satellites/jwst/.

Jones, Lauren V. *Stars and Galaxies.* Santa Barbara, Calif.: Greenwood Press, 2010.

National Aeronautics and Space Administration. "Astrophysics Focus Areas: Dark Energy, Dark Matter." http://science.nasa.gov/astrophysics/focus-areas/what-is-dark-energy/.

National Geographic. "Space: Galaxies." http://science.nationalgeographic.com/science/space/universe/galaxies-article.html.

National Research Council Committee for a Decadal Survey of Astronomy and Astrophysics. *New Worlds, New Horizons in Astronomy and Astrophysics.* Washington, D.C.: National Academies Press, 2010.

Raymo, Chet. *365 Starry Nights: An Introduction to Astronomy for Every Night of the Year.* Englewood Cliffs, N.J.: Prentice-Hall, 1982.

Zirker, J. B. *The Magnetic Universe: The Elusive Traces of an Invisible Force.* Baltimore, Md.: Johns Hopkins University Press, 2009.

McLEAN COUNTY UNIT #5
105-CARLOCK

INDEX